Sequoyah

CHERRY LAKE PRESS

Published in the United States of America by Cherry Lake Publishing Group
Ann Arbor, Michigan
www.cherrylakepublishing.com

Reading Adviser: Beth Walker Gambro, MS, Ed., Reading Consultant, Yorkville, IL
Book Designer: Jennifer Wahi
Illustrator: Jeff Bane

Photo Credits: page 5: © MattRuffmanPhotography/Shutterstock; page 7: © Royal Graphics/Shutterstock; page 9: © Grzegorz Zdziarski/Shutterstock; pages 11, 13: © Morphart Creation/Shutterstock; pages 15, 22: otnaydur/Shutterstock; page 17: Library of Congress; pages 19, 23: © ANUVAT SIRINET/Shutterstock ; page 21: Architect of the Capitol

Cherry Lake Press is an imprint of Cherry Lake Publishing Group.

Library of Congress Cataloging-in-Publication Data

Names: Thiele, June, author. | Bane, Jeff, 1957- illustrator.
Title: Sequoyah / written by: June Thiele ; illustrated by: Jeff Bane.
Description: Ann Arbor, Michigan : Cherry Lake Publishing, [2023] | Series: My itty-bitty bio | Includes index. | Audience: Grades K-1 | Summary: "This biography for early readers examines the life of Sequoyah, the first person to create Cherokee Syllabary, or Cherokee alphabet, in a simple, age-appropriate way that helps young readers develop word recognition and reading skills. Includes table of contents, author biography, timeline, glossary, index, and other informative backmatter. The My Itty-Bitty Bio series celebrates diversity, covering women and men from a range of backgrounds and professions including immigrants and individuals with disabilities"-- Provided by publisher.
Identifiers: LCCN 2022042699 | ISBN 9781668920190 (paperback) | ISBN 9781668919170 (hardcover) | ISBN 9781668922859 (pdf) | ISBN 9781668921524 (ebook)
Subjects: LCSH: Sequoyah, 1770?-1843--Juvenile literature. | Cherokee Indians--Biography--Juvenile literature. | Cherokee language--Alphabet--Juvenile literature. | Cherokee language--Writing--Juvenile literature. | Tennessee--Biography--Juvenile literature.
Classification: LCC E99.C5 S389125 2023 | DDC 973.04/975570092 [B]--dc23/eng/20220912
LC record available at https://lccn.loc.gov/2022042699

Printed in the United States of America
Corporate Graphics

About the author: June Thiele writes and acts in Chicago where they live with their wife and child. June is Dena'ina Athabascan and Yup'ik, Indigenous cultures of Alaska. They try to get back home to Alaska as much as possible.

About the illustrator: Jeff Bane and his two business partners own a studio along the American River in Folsom, California, home of the 1849 Gold Rush. When Jeff's not sketching or illustrating for clients, he's either swimming or kayaking in the river to relax.

I was born in Tennessee around 1775. My mother was **Cherokee**. My father was White.

I had two names. My **Native American** name was Sequoyah. My other name was George Gist.

What other names do you go by?

I spoke Cherokee. It was the only language I knew. At the time, it wasn't a **written language**.

I wanted to make Cherokee into a written language. I wanted to create our own alphabet to write.

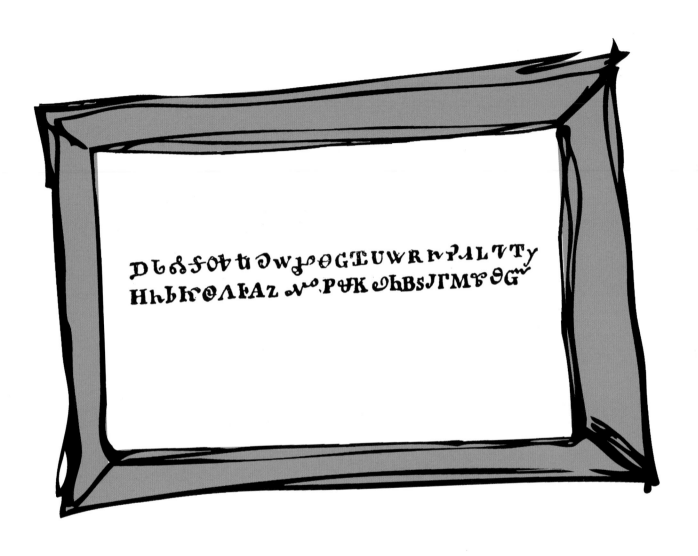

Not everyone liked this. My people said it went against our beliefs. But I knew it was important. I kept working.

13

I finally finished the alphabet in 1821. My daughter helped me. She was only 6 at the time! Next, I taught my brother-in-law.

Cherokee was the first written Native American language. At first, my people didn't like the alphabet. But I convinced them of its usefulness.

ᎦᏬᎥ ᏥᎶᎢᎤᎣᎯ

CHEROKEE PHŒNIX, AND INDIANS' ADVOCATE.

PRINTED UNDER THE PATRONAGE, AND FOR THE BENEFIT OF THE CHEROKEE NATION, AND DEVOTED TO THE CAUSE OF INDIANS—E. BOUDINOTT, EDITOR.

VOL. II. NEW ECHOTA, WEDNESDAY APRIL 7, 1830. **NO. 51.**

PRINTED WEEKLY BY
JNO. F. WHEELER,

At $2.50 if paid in advance, $3 in six months, or $3 50 if paid at the end of the year.

To subscribers who can read only the Cherokee language the price will be $2.00 in advance, or $2.50 to be paid within the year.

Every subscription will be considered as continual unless subscribers give notice to the contrary before the commencement of a new year, and all arrearages paid.

Any person procuring six subscribers, and becoming responsible for the payment, shall receive a seventh gratis.

Advertisements will be inserted at seventy-five cents per square for the first insertion, and thirty-seven and a half cents for each continuance, longer ones in proportion.

☞ All letters addressed to the Editor, post paid, will receive due attention.

The territory of the four southwestern tribes of Indians lies within what are called the chartered limits of Georgia, Alabama, Mississippi, Tennessee, and North Carolina. The portion in the two last named, is small. For the sake of distinctness, and to avoid unnecessary prolixity, your Memorialists would ask the attention of Congress to the case of the Cherokees especially; though the same principles, with immaterial variations, will apply to other Indian communities.

The Cherokee nation of Indians is a distinct community yet remaining of the numerous original inhabitants of this continent. At the first settlement of the Southern States, these natives were found in possession of the lands, which they now occupy. We need not here agitate the question, whether civilized men may appropriate to themselves a newly discovered country, unoccupied except by the occasional visits of migratory hunters. It does not appear that the Cherokees were ever migratory people. They doubtless made excursions...

...sidered as being, a *nation*; but they actually exercise every one of those powers, which we had enumerated, in the declaration of Independence, as the highest attributes of national sovereignty.

By the federal Constitution, the treaty making power was vested in the President and Senate of the United States, and the several States were inhibited from exercising it.— Soon after the constitution went into operation, the first President of the United States with the aid of his very able cabinet, & with the sanction of a Senate, more than one third of whose members were members of the Convention that formed the Constitution, laid the foundation of our present relations with the Indians. In no part of his administration are the proofs of his wisdom and circumspection more apparent. The Indian communities, residing within the limits of the peace of 1783, were implicitly admitted to be distinct communities, and the territory of the Indians was described as "belonging to them," and as not being under the jurisdiction of the legislative or judicial functions of the United...

...racy and rapine, permit a nation to despise its engagements."

Your Memorialists, in pursuing this investigation, find a renewal of the guaranty to the Cherokees, made seven years after it was first given; and in this renewal, the guaranty is declared to be "forever," which was obviously the meaning. In the first instance. In the progress of numerous subsequent negotiations, the Cherokees yielded to the United States the free navigation of the rivers in the Cherokee nation; and made several specific grants of roads through their country, as the progress of white population led the Presidents of the United States to solicit these privileges.

In the late treaty between the United States and the Cherokees,—a compact which was negotiated at Washington, eleven years ago, it is stipulated, that the provisions of the intercourse law, which was made for the protection of the Indians generally, shall be continued for the security of the Cherokees; and thus the provisions of the intercourse law became, in fact, a part of the treaty...

...question of right should be first settled. If this can be clearly ascertained, it should be firmly established. The suggestions of friendship should come afterwards. If the Cherokees have a perfect right to remain where they now are, as long as they please, and to claim the protection of the United States against encroachments from every quarter, they should be told so, in a firm and decisive tone; and the United States should honorably redeem their numerous and solemn pledges.

If the Government, in a spirit of sincere kindness and friendship, should advise the Cherokees to remove, let the Cherokees weigh the advice and decide upon it, as they think best. The question should be freely decided by them, and not by strangers.

But as this question of supposed benevolence does in fact sway the minds of some, so that they cannot fairly look at the question of right, your Memorialists feel bound to say, that they have seen no reason, which satisfy them, that the removal of the Cherokees would be for their benefit.

If the country west of the territory...

Soon, people were teaching the alphabet in schools. Our language was being printed in books and newspapers.

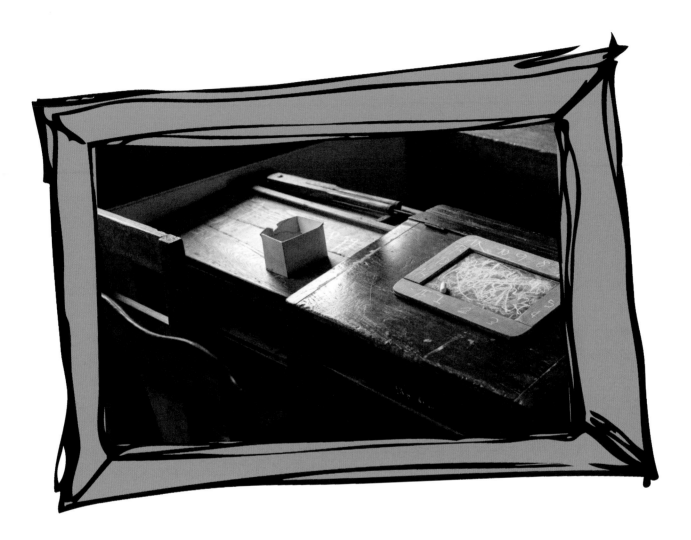

I died in 1843, but my **legacy** lives on. The Cherokee alphabet is still used today.

What would you like to ask me?

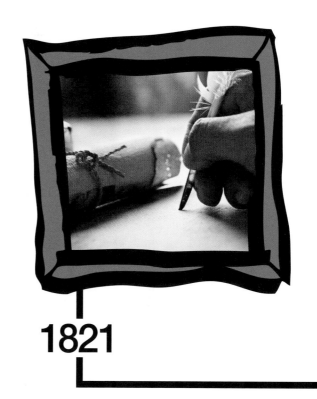

1821

1760

↑
Born
1775

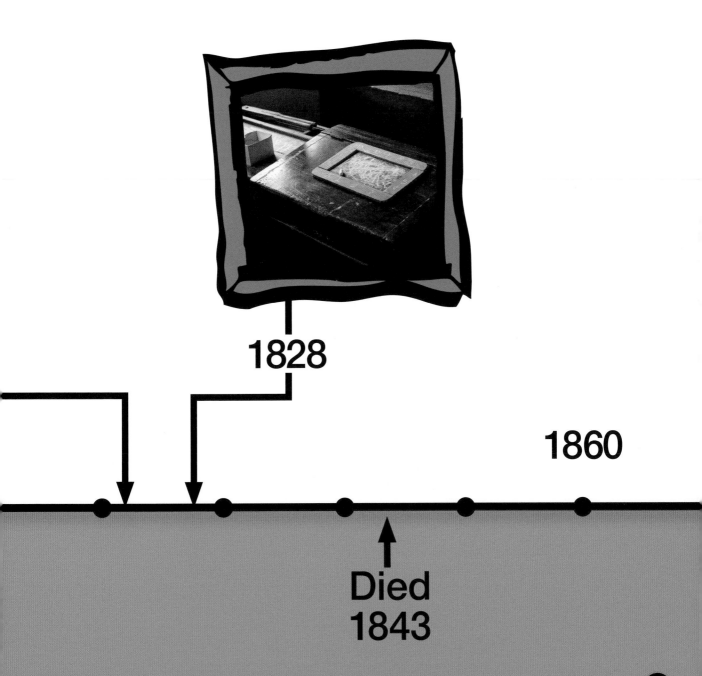

1828

1860

Died
1843

glossary

Cherokee (CHAYR-uh-kee) a member of a North American people originally of the southeastern United States, now with reservations in Oklahoma and North Carolina and living in many different places

legacy (LEH-guh-see) something handed down from one generation to another

Native American (NAY-tiv uh-MEHR-uh-kuhn) one of the people who originally lived on the land that became the United States, or a relative of these people

written language (RIH-tuhn LAN-gwij) written form of communication

index